This book is in two parts. The first part, *You*, is more of my materiel on the ***Reader's Road to Realization***. The second, *Me*, is my Origin Story. Destiny is thus.

Hello Reader,

I need to ask you why Reader, it is that you are reading. One of the reasons, perhaps among many, **must be** that you find the idea of getting to know a superior version of yourself somewhat, if not greatly appealing. Why is this necessary? I'll tell you later. For now, decide, that you, Reader, are going to be who you truly are, based on what you truly want. And that this superior version of you already knows one thing about who you truly are and what you want… That you, Reader, are someone who is (truly) a *Reader*, (which is who you are, based on your actions), and what you truly want, is to find a superior version of yourself.

So read on!

See, we are making progress.

Chapter 1

Introduction

Before proceeding beyond the list of terms, be certain (which is to have no doubt) about wanting to change. Be sure that progress is something that you, Reader want. Allowing the Reader to make progress along their *Roads*, and deriving fulfillment along the way is the purpose of this text. If you truly want something, it must be in accordance with who you truly are. If, in fact, you are truly someone who wants to find a superior version of yourself, through action & change, and knowing who it is you are, then *expectations* and *judgements* must be avoided. If you have any doubt about change, and therefore doubt that you, Reader, would be able to act in accordance with who you are, realize that no personal change can be forced or not undone. Realizing your destiny is at hand. Uncertainty, anxiety, doubt or butterflies present, in your stomach, say, means you are better off stopping everything, sitting down if possible, and **waiting** for direction or certainty, and possibly wisdom, and/ or understanding, if not, humility through shame, for example.

~Chapter 2:

List Of Terms & Symbols

1) ~ : The tilde. In formal logic, this symbol is used to indicate a negative condition of a premise when deriving validity and soundness. In this text, Reader, I will be using it to indicate the lack of presence of a thing. For example ~Judge. It is not the case, Reader, that it is required of you to not judge, it is the case, in fact, Reader, that we must simply not act in conflict to items on our list: Our actions must be, and will be, derived from who we are, and what we want. If ~Judge is on your list, then you will never initiate an event, based on a judgement, given you maintain self control, while living your life.

By ~Control, I mean that given that our actions must be derived from who we are, and that who we are is finite and imperfect, we must never assume we are in control (of anything), or similarly, able to control (anything).

2) Peace or Peacefulness. If one finds one's self thinking, or acting undesirably, the first thing to do is stop and <u>revert</u> to a peaceful emotional state. Practice Peace.

3) Green Pastures. You remember feeling as if lying down in the sun, in green grass, close to calm water. We have all felt peace at one time or another, for some duration. Practice makes *perfect*. Is that fearlessness and understanding there too? [Psalm 23]

4) Wait. It is preferable to wait, and maintain, or revert back to a favorable way of being, rather then allow thought or ~facts or fears: weakness, to determine action.

5) House of Cards: Imagine each ~fact in your mind. One's perception of reality is made up of many, many pieces. Each piece is a fact or ~fact. Being a part of a reality, built of ~facts,

is as if living in a reality, made up of playing cards, on a table with two point two legs, in the wind, on the sand, in the rain.

6) Blind man's cane: Logic

7) Schism: Schism between mind and body & Two-Mindedness, or a rift or fissure between one's thoughts, and one's actions.

8) Listening & Obeying: Being a servant. Humble and meek.

9) The shaving off of excess self. Bits of self make up who we are. Some of these bits are desirable. If a bit of self is ~desirable, which is to say unknown, or undesirable, it should be dragged into the Light, and excised, if negative or superfluous.

10) Ego is fear: Indeed. What prideful feeling is not to cover fear? What do you have to be afraid of?

11) Rejoicing & Mourning: When pride sets in

12) Certainty: Certainty requires the deconstruction, or (idealy) demolition of one's house of cards.

13) List: Proper effort put into your list, will generate your destiny and fulfillment, clearly.

Add to it. Make *Lists* based on actions.
Develop new activities for the sake of refining
your *List* and therefore living your destiny. Try
new lemonade recipes.

14) Agency. Agency here, shpuld be understood
as the ability to shape things around you.
Feelings of clarity and certainty, bring about
notions of things like destiny, agency and
eternity.

15) The arrow released from the bow.

- Knowing Who You Are, and what You want.
- Being projected down your path as a result.

16) ~Judge. Due largely due to every humans
trait of ~perfect, one must not judge. Do not
judge ANYTHING! At all!! The key to
forgiveness is no judgements.

17) ~Expectations. Similar to ridding one's self of
all judgement, is the removal of expectations.
Due largely, if not entirely to, imperfection,
we must not have expectations, for we do not
understand, by our imperfect nature. We are
simple. We are fools.

18) Prudence. When we have accepted we are
imperfect, perhaps largely due to shame, felt

perhaps after actions which were in conflict with who You are, and what You want, despite being (let's say), in the, or a, desirable state of mind, we must be prudent: Be careful of our imperfect nature. Love **nothing** (but God), **more** than You. There is no limit to (amounts of) Love. We are our own worst enemies. We must walk on eggshells around ourselves. See yourself from behind: from a third-person view, omitting superfluous surroundings, asking ourselves only, what's this mook gunna do next?!. We are indeed the same (insert synonym for garbage) as one and another. And before honor, is humility. We must detach from ourselves, as if convinced we stand to… get triggered, at any time. Can you imagine seeing yourself from a third person view? Waiting is prudent. If you have any doubt or two-mindedness or even fear about a situation, sit: wait. Essentially the idea is: You are in a state of grace (optimistically & possibly), why mess it up?! Sit down. Rejoice… Feel the peace. Proceed when certain.

19) Understanding comes to those who have wisdom. Honour with wisdom. Wisdom with prudence. Strength with Understanding (unobtainable to humans, by nature, without counsel.)

20) Fear is incompatible with peacefulness. Ego is fear. Fear of death ends with living your destiny.

21) A little knowledge is a dangerous thing: Do not become satisfied.

22) **Fulfillment** is obtained when one achieves along one's path. It is required, Reader, in this acquisition of fulfillment, that one's *List* contains items which provide these things, when acted out.

At minimum:

   a) One's experience, and path, makes one uniquely suited for something. Let's call it being *one*. If one is to be one, then enough of one's actions need to reflect who one is, and what one wants. There does seem to be a minimum that your actions have to represent you, before any perceived benefit. Couple ~Expectations & ~Judgements. Which is to say, the complete collection of things which have ever happened to one, added to one's destiny, without expectations & judgment, must be aligned with one's actions.

The more, actions of this kind, the merrier.

b) One's actions must, at a minimum, provide fascination, and therefore real personal interest to **practice**, and **theoretically** perfect and perform as reflex.

c) One's actions, to a minimum (personal) amount, must benefit others.

d) One's total actions must be enough to somehow cover minimum living expenses. Sprinkle profitability into actions.

It is also nice to remember that, our actions, if derived from our experiences, and who we are, make us really good at some things, and less so at others.

Finding actions to do, of such a nature, is to find actions that validate your existence, and that you are really good at.

Eyes up on the   Table

Of Contents

~Chapter 1: Introduction

~Chapter 2: List of Terms & Symbols

Chapter 1: Unsure, or Worse? First

Chapter 2: YOUR **LIST**

Chapter 3: **PEACE**

Chapter 4: Deez Words

~Chapter 3: Conclusion

Chapter 5: Part 2: You Me Destiny

There Is No Chapter 6

Chapter ~1: INTRODUCTION

Chapter ~2: Nocking The Arrow

Chapter ~3: The Red Switch

Chapter ~4: Boot Camp

Chapter ~5: Conclusion 2

Chapter 7: More Manifestations

Chapter 1: Unsure, or Worse? First

Readers!

If you find yourself stressed, unsure or worse, first, **wait** & Retreat to **peace**. Second & third: **Do not judge** – anything & Have **no expectations.** This means of others, yourself, God, reality, the universe: Anything. You have no control over the universe – Yield. If at any time, including presently, you find yourself feeling or thinking (undesirably), simply wait. Feel peace. Imagine a checklist with three items on it: Peacefulness, ~Judgements & ~Expectations.

Imagine checking them off. Imagine red check marks appearing in the vertically listed, big green boxes.

1) Wait. Then Retreat to Green Pastures: Retreat to Peace.

2) Do not judge – anything.

3) You have no control over the universe – Have no expectations. Yield. When you perceive the items on the list getting checked off, you should also imagine yourself getting into a ready position, like that of a fighter, with his hands up, ready for anything (based on choice, repetition and individuality). While in such a frame-of-mind, one can react to possibly randomly occurring, unforeseeable events, based on who you are, and what you want. It is, in fact only possible to react to something, based on the frame of mind one is in, at the moment any event occurs.

Chapter 2: YOUR **LIST**

YOUR **LIST**

Let us therefore, from now on, be conscious of our *__List__* of things that represent Who We Are. Items which are placed on this list are not actively pursued, instead, after we have acted, we must ask ourselves if the items on our list have been respected. If so, or if not, why. Removal of a list item, among other things, brings one closer to their True self. So, start adding 'em!

The first thing, which we kind of already added, is a **Reader** of this text. The second thing, that we all are, is imperfect. This can also be represented by ~Perfect.

Also add ~Judge & ~Expectations to your list.

What is it we must know about being imperfect? Well, that for better or for worse, nothing we ever do can be perfect, or can even remain what it is, infinitely. Though I consider it slightly redundant, it is the case that your *List* of things that represents you, can never actually have too many aspects on it, just the desirable, and undesirable. Let us therefore

Add ~infinite to your *List*.

Adding and removing traits to your list, while being aware, honest and open about your actions, can generate fulfillment, given a goal of yours is to realize superior versions of yourself, along your *road*. Remove things from your *List* if they are not presently representing who you are, when considering what it is that you want. Always add list items to, or back to your List if your actions dictate it. Remember, you are your actions. Do not deny your experience, and therefore your abilities, Reader.

A good exercise, then, one can occupy one's self with, as part of one's road to greater realization, is to add things to your *List*. Then, as if they did actually represent you, based on what you want, you need to, naturally, act on them. The more items you can leave on your list, the easier it should be to be fulfilled. The more personal list items you can incorporate into an *action*, or event, the greater the likelihood of fulfillment. There seems to be no upper max limit to fulfillment, once the threshold has been crossed.

Similarly, after acting, one can examine the items that others would say are on your list, which you will hopefully be open enough to see (if there). List items are generated, as well, involuntarily as a result of actions. If one is one's actions, then you, Reader, may be a whole bunch of things you not only don't potentially realize, but a bunch of things you would not say represent who you truly are.

*Wait.

*Peace.

*READY POSITION: (~Judge & ~Expectations) + (*List* items)

…

Proceed

Chapter 3: **PEACE**

Peace, like anything, is not simply ours to simply possess, and fully comprehend, any or all of the time. Imperfection is at the center of life, regardless. We cannot through personal, human understanding alone, hope to be anything, indefinitely. I will proceed from the notion, however, that all people can access and feel peace, by nature. It's hard to imagine that it could be so simple: it's hard to imagine that not only are we all in possession of peace, but that we always have been, and it's only injustice and our imperfection which prevents us from perceiving it.

Try, Reader, to remember a time you felt peaceful. Perhaps you were lying in green grass, beside some still water. Regardless, the fact that you can seemingly feel peacefulness, theoretically at will, has got to fascinate you. The first item to check off, when concerned about one's state of mind, is Peace.

Consider if one were to be at peace, and was as if **the arrow, that springs from the bow.** Before one can sail to their target, a bow must be built: a specialized task one must undertake, analogous to being a Reader of this book. Next, one must take aim: prepare for the task ahead (your life), and then simply, sail to your inevitable destination. Anything as insignificant as dust, or as solid as a person, between you, and for that matter, around above under or beside you, and your target, is, like you are, in precisely the right place, at precisely the right time. Therefore, anything expected or otherwise, that occurs or effects anything perceivable, or otherwise, anywhere, at any time, between you and your target (between you and your destiny), once you are on your way, must be occurring exactly as it should, when it should, regardless of your understanding of why it should.

Additionally, mathematically, it would seem the chance or probability that others around you, regardless of their intent, could get caught up in (your) destiny. It stands to reason, if you, Reader, are living your true destiny, and someone interacts with you, the probability they will be able to interact with their destiny could only increase. This can be a great reassurance for you, when others, and their enduring dissatisfaction are at hand.

So… Charles… How did you figure any of this out, and why should I not take you for a quack? Well, Reader, who has skeptic on their *List*, currently, in order for me to illuminate you, I would only ask that you, and all Readers, reading these words, to now expand your *List*, once again. Always keeping in mind what this *List* is. It is a *List* of things which represent you, and are items not in conflict with what it is you in fact want. Therefore, to prevent schism, we must DO & BE the things on the *List*.

Add now, It is not the case that you are in, or have control: ~Control.

Next, let us add both good & servant, for they are worth exploring and difficult, at first.

Let's also plant a seed of creativity:

Add Considers the impossible

The greatest among you, will be servants.

It does, however, occur to me, after working through this material with others, that obeying is not something, let's say, many people I know, do very easily. It turns out that in order to obey: be as a servant, one must hear and not add to a command, or an idea, vocally, mentally, or otherwise. Try to navigate the world with zero analysis, even **of** your senses. Your brain, which I will compare to a computer, only has a finite amount of processing power. This power, you might imagine is analogous to RAM. The idea would be, that as soon as your computer processes any information, it becomes a contaminated subject, through your imperfection, and you have just limited other, desired processes. The contaminant is your desires, perceptions, fears and ego: the Darkness.

Chapter 4: Deez Words

Deez Words, mark the next steps, in the right direction on the right path, to the rest of your life. Let's all take a breath and rejoice, and find some peace in this moment, for not many things are more rewarding, it seems, then knowing who you are, and what you want.

Our Road, is not something that you can simply hop on to, but something that you have to perceive, and eventually find yourself on. I use the word perception, because everyone has a perception of reality. Everyone has assumptions, beliefs, facts, emotions, and so on, which make up their reality. I assert that deez realities are analogous to standing about in a house build out of playing cards. This house, which is susceptible to the slightest of winds, criticisms, whispers which cause confusion, or even deliberate attack, fares not well without one's undivided attention, which most are seemingly fine with. Most people seem content to spend much of their time simply defending their already standing- barely, facts of their reality: their cards which make up their house, fortress or tower of cards. They defend their cards with their logic. Even if one can repel attacks and prevent the outside world from getting in, you are still living in flimsy excuses for facts, built upon sand. The sand of your fathers. Sand, not next to still water no, but sand of the ocean and of the tide. Regardless of how it makes you think or feel, Reader, the tide is coming in. All of our houses of cards, we must realize, if we would like to be happier, and more fulfilled, that to be less controlled by anxiety and therefore less occupied with depression, is to bring the cards down. It is simply a matter of controlling one's fear, and therefore ego, along with judgement & expectations. Once fear, for the purpose of being who one wants, is eliminated, through identification, certainty, despite one's perceptions, reactions and emotions can be felt and maintained. As this can be done, and like the other things on the *List*, is only (fully) achieved if one's actions reflect, in this case, fearlessness: the things on one's *List*.

... Guess what! Time to edit your *List*!

1. Add Fearless.
2. Add Does not set conditions for failure OR success
3. Add: Does listen! or ~~listen. Next,
4. Add ~(brain processing power occupied with depression)

… If one feels such a thing, or anxiety, doubt or regret, we can now work on our *Lists* instead. We can now find certainty. Wait!! We can now feel peace, and check off boxes. We can now be the arrow that springs from the bow.

Wait, if not certain or unsure of how to proceed down your path. Feel the peace.

Now, we need to discuss some, potentially rough words. It may be.. . difficult to maintain your ready position, in order to listen/ read on, but, two things. First, that this therefore will be a good exercise for you, Reader, along with any other event, which occurs, which potentially effects you or your actions:

could jeopardize who you are, based on your actions: practice.

Who are you? What do you want? For, to be a Reader of this text, I must stress, is to be open. Open to possibilities. And perseverance breeds experience. Experience, however, certainly requires action. So, given you, Reader, require of yourself that you act in accordance with who you truly are, and therefore will have experience based on who you truly are, do not fear the unknown or incorrect… or anything else… as that's not who you are anymore.

The first word is faith

The second is openness.

Add Openness, or Is Open, or ~~Open to your *List*.

This won't be a problem, as I must ask all Readers of this text to have some faith… in the author of this text, on the subject of this text, Reader, as to do otherwise would be a waste.

If you can do this: if you can put faith in something besides yourself, if only just the author of a book you are presently reading, for the sake of better understanding the (my) ideas, you can persevere. You will gain experience. It may be quite illogical for you to consider, and therefore very difficult, but are you not a Reader of this text, intent on overcoming yourself, with ideas and derived actions otherwise unknown and untried? Indeed…

If faith can be put in the future, and in one's true abilities, then, anxiety, depression, doubt and regret, along with fear, ego and unwanted self, will be a thing of your past. They are things, certainly, relatively, largely in my past. It's seemingly very difficult to stay, call it focused. But it's not poor focus that burdens us, poor focus is incidental of the underlying condition ~Perfect. As we are discussing how to simply live the way we truly want, given imperfection, derived from who we truly are, we all must constantly be aware of the fact that, the way we normally do, or the things that represent us today, cannot in fact be a perfect representation of who you are and what you want, given, again, imperfection. To seek a superior version of ourselves, is to be certain of our own ignorance. With wisdom is honour. Before honour is humility. The Reader must understand that it is a destructive process that I am suggesting, one I have greatly enjoyed due in part, certainly, to the benefits of the destruction, as well as the process. If you can see a superior life for yourself, through identifying a more true version of yourself, through knowing who you are (knowing your *List*), and what you want, it stands to reason, that whatever *it is:* your life *is*, that you will need a superior self.

Now, at first, you might say, *Okay, sure. Sounds great.* Obviously it's not always easy. Sometimes it will be hard. Accepting change requires faith. Whether or not you, Reader, at this moment realize that it is in fact fear, which generates ego, and that ego is ~Good. Perhaps it is that you, Reader, are simply overly egotistical, and perhaps you even think that you're adequate, or more than adequate, or, you know, something that sounds like, *reality is lucky to have me around.* If you are in fact a Reader of this text, I would hope, nay, I would demand that you have faith. Have faith in me, and my notion that fear breeds ego. We use ego to defend our perceived realities: our house of cards. What is also fascinating, and critical, is that selfishness is not desirable. That true goodness, is only performed in the absence of selfishness. So,

Add ~Selfish to your *List*, along with

Add ~egotistical

This should be getting fun.

For you, Reader, are interested in rising up out of the flames, like the phoenix, stronger and better than ever, after having destroyed a past, less desirable version of yourself.

Most things that I discuss, will require adopting or developing skills as part of your path, to understanding and knowing yourself: who it is you are, and what it is you want. Keep in mind that a great deal of what life is, is getting to know yourself better, over time, through time. Skills are a result of proficiency. Proficiency can only be obtained through action and experience. It is, which is to say life is going to be mostly like training yourself to do some task. Like, brush your teeth. And the idea would be the more you do it, the better you would get at it, the more comfortable you would be with it, the easier it will be to remember, the more likely it will be that you develop something like muscle memory, for your behavior: desirable reactions. Practice makes perfect, and what we are talking about here, is practicing being You. Experiment with it, mess around with it, whatever. The idea is that whenever you test your concept of who it is you are, the result would be knowledge and likely a strengthening of your faith.

We will go from whoever you are now, conceptualized as a point on a line, to where you want to be. Wherever you want to be, is known through knowledge of who you are: knowledge of a truer version of yourself, and what you truly want. Creativity is considering and doing the impossible.

Now seems an appropriate time to reveal my thoughts on writing a book. The purpose of a book, of this book, is salvation. Yours, Reader, and therefore mine. I wish to allow as many humans as possible to feel peacefulness, as a means of relieving anxiety, on a path to Self, certainty and destiny. As many as possible as quickly as possible. It shall be stipulated that those who pass this trial: those who persevere, and generate relevant experiences… Evolution come out the other side. Better understanding of who it is you are, and what you want, shall generate your destiny, shall generate certainty and momentum …

~Chapter 3: Conclusion

Reader,

Add to your *List*:

 Are/Am (The arrow that springs from the bow).

Those who emerge. The arrow, and sail along their path, no doubt, no regret, no looking back necessary, no hesitation, will achieve something. What you, Reader achieve, will depend on your actions. Do they represent who you are and what you want? Or not?!

Chapter 5: Part 2: You Me Destiny

Thank You, Reader, for checking out the first part of this book: *You*. Here is the *Me* part. It covers what some might call my Rebirth. Our paths converging is destiny.

Hello again, Reader!

My name is Charles Cummings, I am 35, and I have been Christian since April 2020. I did go to McGill University in Montreal, Quebec, Canada, and end up with a psychology degree from Carleton University, which is to say I am not a complete quack. I was certainly not Christian until last year. My story of going from a perceived life of depression, anxiety, and logic, to one of joy, destiny and the Spirit, is, a fabulous one. Get your **List** out, Reader, this is gunna be Good.

"Logic is the blind man's cane. It can get you through your day, without dying."

- Charles "is Cool" Cummings

Chapter ~1: INTRODUCTION

Try having faith, I did.

Imagine a life

Where every day could be considered lesser than the last.

One way this could happen

Is if each day is perceived as similar enough to receive the same score on ten.

If every day is the same, each rerun, though similar, is less brilliant than the last.

Add the fact that the perceived score of your day has, in fact, been declining, certainly over time, and is scored in your mind around a negative 37 gajillian.

There's this term "rock bottom."

Fortunately, and unfortunately, there is no top or bottom to this scale.

It is all perception.

When on a negative day quality trajectory, one may wait to hit rock bottom, perhaps secretly tired of declining day quality.

On the way up, it is easier to see the day quality graph for what it is:

Way better for happy people.

The folks on their way down are waiting, not in green pastures with understanding, minus fear. No.

They wait for change, without changing.

I'm not in some sort of position to say which way of living is better

And obviously no two people's lives are identical,

So imagine there are a specific, finite amount of paths one can walk

And each path, here, is a destiny

Zero one two or twenty million people can walk any given path.

There is one path of dust. I had been walking it for more than thirty three years.

No two (individuals) are the same.

I can say I have been on more than one path

I can say that some are more or less desirable,
based on who I am and what I want.

Things I would call negative are undesirable

Things I would call positive are desirable

There is no limit to either (any?) side of the graph.

Imagine being more and more fulfilled every day.

Imagine that each step, literally, can bring fulfillment.

Imagine loving yourself, and everything else, more
and more, each day.

Imagine the opposite.

Decide you're done

With perception

Any word's meaning is decided on by us

Individually. So you need to find out who you are and
what you want

So you can omit negativity: that which is not
desirable.

Omit:

Anger, stress, indecision, regret, depression, doubt, fear, judgement, unwanted thought, unwanted perception, definitions, terms for failure & success, greed, hate, envy, ………

See who you are, by knowing what you want

Why not try a bunch of stuff?

Can you wait?

Stop.

Wait.

Feel the peace

Know who you are

Be prudent

Annnnd fire!

   By what I remember, I found out a sufficient amount about who I truly am, and what I truly wanted, by March 14th, 2020, to project me on a path, which eventually ledd me to this path: The Path of

Righteousness. Realistically, the change to who I was occurred at least a day or two earlier, but I likely did not let myself admit it right away. Perceiving happiness, love and or fulfillment, and a bunch of other awesome stuff, with expectations, can be debilitating. This fear can easily be caused by past perceived heartbreak, or undesirable circumstances. I realized, on March 14th, 2020, that all depression was gone, along with what I would have said was 80% of my anxiety. I told NO ONE for a fortnight. On the 28th, I told my sister and mom & dad, and a couple people online, that two weeks ago I was free from depression and most anxiety. The reaction I wanted, I did not get.

As the arrow, on my path, I told myself that the reactions I got, were exactly the ones I was supposed to get, regardless of whether I understood why. This is generally a great attitude to have. Omit anger etc… The next day in the car with my folks driving, I saw the reaction I wanted, when we got four green lights in a row: A lot of awe and pointing.

Expectations, I was realizing more and more, along with judgment, are at the center of many undesirable circumstances and actions. The reason I tried not to think about it, or mention it, had to do with two factors. First, the reactions of others, at that time, already meant the proper amount to me. Secondly, the fact that when I perceived a lack of depression and most anxiety, I thought it was likely that I was dreaming or completely nuts. This would be good practice.

Chapter ~2:

Nocking The Arrow

I argue, that if everyone is an arrow, then I spent 33 plus years lying on the ground, collecting dust. What I in fact set out to find, for certainly not the first time, was a life where the things I did, I did by choice, where I was happy with life, money and relationships.

Notably, lockdowns, and increased fear and loneliness, by January 2020, was a reality. As such, my depression and anxiety were at an all-time high. I decided some time around then, that I was going to get busy living, and that **all** the things, possibly, that I

perceived, believed, was passionate about etc…
were not necessarily as I truly wanted them.

The first, and essentially, only step to me, at that
time, was to figure out who I truly am/ was. From
what I would have described as a rational, scientific
position, I attempted to find out personal character
traits, that I was unaware of, or would simply not
have let myself see. I reflected… and watched
YouTube videos for many hours…

By the 14th of March, 2020, I had added 3 things to
my LIST. I was ready to accept the fact that I was
both interested in **goodness** and **teaching**. Third,
imperfect was glaring me in the face, given I was
what I refer to as miserable, at 34.

The level of … personal imperfection which I
perceived at that time, was significant. Not that such
a thing exists as we imagine it, I would indeed say
that at that time, I had perceived hitting rock bottom.
Though I didn't feel like I knew nothing, I started
acting like it. Perceiving giving up and changing can
generate anxiety, or the opposite. Think about what
that could be. Omit the undesirable.

Long before the word omit would come to my mind to use in this context, I started reminding myself not to think, for "it hadn't really done me any major favours." After major revelation, which occurred by the 14th, I was feeling as if fired, from the bow, sailing surely toward its target. What I did, in order to get to that point: the present, was to decide there was a superior version of myself, which I could find and be. Also that all my knowledge and experience, for 34 years, hadn't produced it. Ironically, perhaps, is how we must never deny our experience, regardless, and that we are our actions.

To feel certainty, we must not doubt that we are in the right place at the right time: We must accept our past. If you feel, likely after a perceived revelation or success, that you are in the right place, at the right time, you can tell yourself surely, that all aspects of your past, right up until now, are exactly as they should be. For if they were not, you could not now be here, exactly as you are. Rejoice, Reader. To feel as if fired from the bow, one must perceive a third point ahead of them. In the future, which could be 3 seconds from now, when that point is reached, and you are in a new present, exactly as it should be, from a past one, a trajectory and line are perceived. If that third point was arrived at by acting based on who you are, Reader, which you have deciphered sufficiently, due to having a true enough idea of what it is, you in fact want, Reader, progress and direction is perceived. Success is experienced. If this was your intent, especially if profitability, in dollars, can be perceived, fulfillment is had. One can organize their life so that, say, every three seconds, they can have more fulfillment.

Before I was able to add any new <u>List</u> items, I had to *shave off self.* It would take until April, (most likely), to learn that term, but I instantly adopted it into my vocabulary. I had started realizing that fear caused ego and false reality. I started realizing that being good, or even nice, required forgiveness and eliminating judgements. Eventually one can omit selfishness. I started exploring more and more aspects of myself I had taken for granted. I shaved and realized, realized and shaved. Sufficient shaving, leads to giving up, or *submission*. I started to accept & see that I was fascinated by philosophical Goodness, righteousness and ethics & morals. I saw and admitted I had always taught others where possible. As time went on, it seemed that I was making progress especially, and perhaps only, when I considered the impossible: assumed I did not know.

It is also the case that finding two new aspects of my self was insufficient to trigger my flight, surely and certainly, down my road. After the three, however, I was so preoccupied with this progress, and by what I would come to call certainty, combined with a sense of ignorance, that I did what seemed very logical at the time.

At this time, I was 34, was suffering from anxiety, depression, was unemployed, single and broke. I have a university degree, that I am still paying for. I had lost confidence in myself. I had never understood faith or thought concepts of God were worth exploring. I knew some would disagree. I would have said I was agnostic. I would have defined that as doesn't believe in God, but can't actually be sure. Fortunately, I had never been crazy about 100% certainty about anything. I knew that I envied Christians for their apparent reduced fear and doubt levels. All this mixed with not wanting to think, due to lost confidence, and an overall admitted ignorance, caused me to start preparing an objective experiment where I would, without expectation, try and learn about what it meant to be an individual with good and teacher on my List. Before I decided on how to approach learning about, and acting on these new List items, I, again, from an agnostic point of view, remembered martial arts, and cooking, for example, where in order to improve and learn, I imitated a master. … After some time I decided to learn about Christianity and Jesus, in order to also learn of righteousness and teaching.

By Sunday March 22nd, 2020, I was ready to start my experiment. The importance and magnitude of actions was starting to present itself to me, and as such, I felt it of paramount importance to actually act out (my perceptions of) my new experimental List items. Prevent *schism*. I took the Jesus List and broke it down somewhat, so as to be sure and not miss learning about any individual concepts I had identified.

I can remember clearly wanting to understand forgiveness for all, loving all equally, faith, and the capitalized, philosophically *True*, concepts, which I was told imperfect humans could not grasp, like Goodness and Righteousness. Months later, I would refer to this assertion that I not only did not currently understand Goodness, and similar concepts, but that such things are from God, and therefore, as a human, that in fact, I could not understand such things as capital G Goodness, as the challenge to my morality. Similarly, morals, ethics and laws, were to be studied from the Christian perspective, whatever that was. I did not own a Bible, or have any intentions of reading one. The only folks I spoke any of this to, were online, and essentially unknown.

So, some time that Sunday, I was feeling as if I had been properly loaded into my bow, (I had assembled a _List_, Reader, I felt represented what Jesus would do), in order to, through acting, learn about Jesus, by acting as he would, or as closely to how I figured he would have, at that time. It is important to note, that at that time, I saw Jesus Christ as just some other human. No additional value or uniqueness did I attach. I had no notion that it would be any more difficult to understand him, than a great martial artist, or chef, for example.

Chapter ~3:

The Red Switch

I was ready. It was Sunday afternoon or evening, and my plan was to simply initiate the experiment, and do some everyday things. I remember, clearly, imagining flipping a big red switch in my mind, from its pre experiment, downward, 0 position, to up, on, and in the 1 position.

As if by reaction to me doing this, I literally perceived being tapped on the shoulder. I don't believe I ever turned my head. I immediately knew what was happening. I would guess I had my first doubt two to three seconds after being poked, and knowing God had done it.

I don't think I froze, exactly, but I thought and moved very little, largely because I would now wonder if I was crazy for a good couple or few months. The state-of-mind I maintained was one of zero expectations. It was objective. To think was to admit I was being irrational. I listened.

I was informed that if I wanted to know of the tools and knowledge of (something like) heaven or the

Light, that I would have to listen, and not assume, and have faith. I actually responded that I did not have or understand faith. I asked if I could borrow some. I received.

I was told, after agreeing on terms, that I had (now), been drafted into the Army of the Light. I was told boot camp started tomorrow. I was pleased.

Now, whatever I was going to do with that day, had been altered. If there is one thing I can say about what happened in that room, before sleep, it is that my tendency to analyze had not been significantly reduced, yet. Oddly, I had faith. Either I was going to have faith, or be crazy. Sleep came quickly.

Chapter ~4:

Boot Camp

When I woke up on Monday, I received. I can't remember if I got time for poop, shower and a shave... Day one, I was informed, was weapons training day one. The first, and most important weapon, I perceived, was God's Love. At that time, I did not know why this love were different from any other. The idea it is applied equally to all is important. No favorites, or selfishness, or expectations, also.

Within an hour or two of… well, returning, I was chatting online, acting out my experiment, without two-mindedness, as much as possible, having conversations about everyone being the same trash and forgiveness, while particularly predisposed with my new love-sword. … Lol

I kept largely to myself that week. Day two, Tuesday was also weapons training. I perceived this weapon as forgiveness, which I would later equate with not judging. Forgiveness to be necessary less than love, made almost irrelevant by judging not. Forgiveness, for humans, is used when judgement has been passed. I conversed some amount with others that day, discussing how it might be possible to forgive anyone, infinitely. Later on I would realize the key to forgiveness is zero judgement. Then, it is for the condemned.

The third day, Wednesday, nothing happened. I had faith. Time passed. I was certain. I did whatever it was that I did that day. I passed: I expected not. I had faith. I would give God's borrowed faith back.

Day four, Thursday, I was given my next tool, what I perceived then as an infinite ammo clip. Thursday was on His plan. I was made to consider principles and truths of the Bible I had never cared for, or given any credit to. A vision of the crucifixion and betrayal was perceived. I learned much. I gained understanding of such stories which I deemed nonsense, like that of Adam and Eve, and Noah's Arc. I am saved. Perhaps I did receive the infinite that day: perhaps I did receive the Spirit that day.

It was Friday. The boot, in this case, took four days. Therefore, there was no arriving at the camp on Friday. On the fifth day, I was required to know my role and enough of what that meant, to maintain my path. I required (shamefully), more, for I did indeed have faith, which is super sweet, but I was, still worried I had gone right out of my mind. Iasked for a miracle. I asked God for a symbol, or an Icon I could have that might represent my cause. This seemed sufficient (to my brain), at that time. I received, once again. It is an image of the flower, which grew up from a seed, amongst the rocks. I think from that moment on, though I have weak moments, I have been Christian.

Chapter ~5:

Conclusion 2

Since that day, I have perceived destiny. Only when overcome by weakness, do I stray from the Righteous path. I perceive such a path by omitting that which is not representative of who I truly am, and what I truly want. Realizing what it is that you truly want, Reader, is a matter of shaving of self, and eventually of submission, death, and rebirth. I write, not with the intention that you become me or lose track of you, Reader, but that through adopting aspects of any or all these ideas, you can enact & manifest a superior, more desirable, more loved (by you), version of yourself, every day, into being. To rid yourself of ego, is to admit & overcome fear. To do unto others, is to not judge, nor have expectations. It is to forgive. It requires listening, trust and love. Omit selfishness, desire, temptation and that which is not of the Light: Be altruistic. To consider **the** path of Righteousness, is to welcome anxiety. Rejoice, Reader. A narrow path implies one where indecision is not present. What a relief. The rewards are better than rubies, yay!!

Chapter 7: More Manifestations

<u>It is the case that</u>

Consider that God would have the trait Perfect on his *List*. Intrinsically, or by nature, this means God perfectly understands all things, as ~finite, or infinite, would also be on His *List*. In order to better understand this, imagine our universe as a circle. Now, imagine a dot outside that circle. That would be where God would (may) exist. From outside our space and time, He created our space and time. Therefore, without time or ignorance restrictions, God would be able to *modify* our universe. One fascinating idea to consider is: If God is all knowing and perfect, how is it possible He could understand that which is not perfect, if one is perfect? I would argue that God did not understand us, and even came to regret our creation, before understanding was bridged by one Spirit, unto the Father. Therefore, The Father's complete, perfect understanding of things which are imperfect is possible, as our understanding of perfection is possible.

<u>cards of House</u>

Now, one of the main processes, or the main goals of this text is to show that each of us has a ~fact collection, or as I call it, a house of cards. This is a way of thinking of the way we deal with life: with reality. The goal of this text, one might say, is to free yourself of the dangers of being within a tower, or on a world composed of thin cardboard playing cards. The issue being, obviously, that at any time, despite your best efforts, you may fall through. We act as if this is normal, and with much of the total effort we expend, we protect our cards, so that the world can keep making sense, in the way we see it making sense. When a card is knocked down, we seek desperately to remedy the situation. It would be very possible for someone to present a problem to your reality and present a solution, with the intent of manipulating. The more you know, the more you know you don't know. This saying became known to me, at roughly, 18, after high school, in what is called CEGEP in Quebec, in Canada, in what was one of my first philosophy classes. This expression and instantly loved it. I thought about it. I memorized it because it's first kind of hard to keep in your head. Tongue twister, not that simple. Here I am, roughly, 17 years later, just recently having figured it out. You, Reader, will have the luxury of someone explaining it as no one ever did to me. To realize what this statement truly means, one must not simply act as is common every time one *learns* something. One generally feels satisfied, realizes *there's more out there to learn*, and that, *Boy! The world and galaxy, and gee wiz! the universe! Is such a never ending source of facts, knowledge, wonder... Wow...* Though that potentially is the case, what this statement means is:

At some point you realize that everything you know is garbage: it's trash. So, when one says "the more you know, the more you know you don't know," one must immediately end all thought, or be considered a hypocrite (if you like the saying...).

Brain Processing Power

It is less possible to do anything well, without full use of one's brain! A great reason for trying to understand this text, and my ideas behind it, Reader, is that I assert that anyone who becomes more adept at acting like themselves, will spend less of their brain processing, overall, conscious or otherwise, on things or subjects which do not represent who they are. What this means, is an increase in velocity down one's road. It means you will feel smarter. This is simply due to less stress and doubt, for example. While living one's destiny, as the arrow, one will doubtlessly be sharper, without unwanted stresses, requiring effort. Imagine, that there is a Reader somewhere who, on average, expends 20% of their brain power on, say doubt and stress. This would mean that, in an hour, of all the things this Reader uses their brain on, 20% of it would stand to not benefit them, or effect them negatively, given doubt and stress do not represent the Reader's true self. To remedy this, is to allocate 20% more brain power to one's destiny. It's thrilling. My brain is freed up for more (miscellaneous) usage. Anxiety, depression, doubt and unwanted emotion, is generally stressful and requires effort. How much effort do you expend on stress? Remember, practice makes perfect. What are you good at, based on who you are?

Feel the Peace

It's what you've been using to get around:

logic is the blind man's cane. This is a good one I came up with. If you, Reader realize the meaning of either of these two statements, it would imply you realize that your perceptions, facts and reality are imperfect and wrong. Realizing such a thing, without being of two minds, Reader, would mean a full submission to your imperfection. It would mean that you would stop building your house of cards. The more I know, the more I know I don't know anything at all. Right. I've learned that the facts that I *know* are really just a substitute for facts.

No Regrets

When you get onto your road, you can be certain that everything you have done led there/ here. And therefore, though it might hurt still, it is not to be regretted. Guilt cannot be had, if we are on our path. Everything that has happened, has brought us to where we are, which is where we need to be to get where we're going, which, among other places is death.

Unknowable Plan

To be without fear of death, one must know why they are living, and that they will die. What happens with belief in your life, is a perceived shortening of your life and a feeling not of fear of death, but instead of not dying your true death. If you were to fall off your road, you could miss your destiny, theoretically.

Part of what we are aiming for, Reader, is what can be called or referred to as "*not thinking.*"

-Arthur O. Facts.

It is obvious that nobody's going to take away your brain or manipulate you or do anything to you while you're simply alone reading this book, or listening to it. So, fear, that may start building up at any time , which may generate anger or other unwanted emotion or actions, is likely due to the difficulty of change. Imagine you have been who you are, for some time, due to consistent actions, which in fact are now, certainly, in contradiction with who you are, and what you want. Since unfortunately, in this case, practice makes perfect, it may be very difficult for one, Reader, to even notice behaviors which are undesirable, because at this point, these actions may not even be perceived as optional. Now we have to get actions which do represent you, in the place of the ones that don't. Imagine acting out of reflex, in such a way that produces fulfillment!

Have you been adding to your *List*?

On Simultaneousness

A moment to remember, that I do remember well, is the time I had the revelation to do with simultaneousness, and finding one's self, on one's road.

If you are certain, Reader, that you

1. Are in the right place at the right time.
2. Want to find your road, and that
3. you have just acted to that effect, (without contradicting what you want, based on who you are), then you can logically and
4. soundly claim that you are in fact on your path.

 When I realized this aspect of finding one's road existed: this aspect involving simultaneousness it would only be two more days until certainty would negate my depression.

Look for me online, Reader!

Fear

Reader, in order to overcome fear, one must see fear for what it is: weakness & imperfection. We must all adopt prudence. Prudence is needed where imperfection is present. We need to keep an eye on ourselves given that, for the sake of this text, Reader, and is seemingly in fact the case, that all egotistical action, is based in fear. Even things like greed and judgment, which can often be linked to the ego, trace back to fear. Things like hate and violence, are all due to fear and fake realities, that receive protecting. If these realities: if these houses of cards receive too many shots, they stand to crumble, which could stand to bring about madness in the individual who loses their cards, without wanting to. They are pretty weak and often little houses or shacks of cards. Sometimes one finds themselves the owner of a tower or castle of cards. The idea is that you, Reader, have protected your house in the past, and will again, (perhaps), just like everyone else. The next time Reader, you hear a thing that would normally anger, or otherwise agitate you, remember that I say that such anger his fear, or ego, or selfishness. Even violence is all a result of fear, just figure it out: work backwards through possible motivations of the action. It is obviously possible that it's not applicable in every situation. However, I think it will be enlightening to explore the possibility.

So, after you wake up, feel good about yourself and then remember about all the times you've done wrong by others. And then, rejoice for all the times that you'll be able to do right by others.

How in the world do you perceive the world without judgment? Well, that's a matter of fear, essentially. Basically, one has to become able to look at something, and not think that you understand it. In fact, it is the case that thinking anything about it, is what we're trying to avoid. With realizing that most of your thoughts are motivated by fear, and that ideas that may have turned out to be perceived as positive, are not only not what they seem, but that these ideas and things are very very very very likely incomplete, incorrect, and are themselves or are composed of those things which we knowingly, or otherwise, use to derive other undesirable conclusions and things that your ego prevents you from truly seeing. For, if it wasn't for your ego, then fear would overcome you. .. This is a great deception So, once you can look at stuff without assessing it, then maybe you can start assessing it properly. However, there does seem to be an order to these things, which I feel is largely based on one's expectations of all things one has perceived. If this seems like an oversimplification, you make things, as your own worst enemy, unnecessarily difficult for yourself.

If this seems like an impossibility, your perceptions and fear and therefore ego have rendered you close minded. It's your life. Your perceptions, problems, concerns and everything else, are flawed, of the flesh and likely pointless or worse. They are supported by the ego, and by weakness or imperfection-based perceptions of things which make everything seem more dire than they are.

Interactions & Chaos

Interactions with the world can be classified under human and non human. Things which are human are people. People, in this sense are the things which make them who they are. Examples of such things are personalities, feelings, (arguably) souls, genetics and all the other stuff, like their complete *List* of experiences. Non human things, therefore everything else, including the things that individuals do and effect, are a second classification of thing we can refer to as chaos. Because our actions represent who we are, and because we all want to be who we truly want to be, our reactions with the human, inhuman, known and unknown aspects of chaos can be controlled by limiting the amount of possible reactions that we have to every possible situation.

First, the human interaction. The key to mastering interactions with others, and the situations generated by them, hypothetical or otherwise, is credited to one's lack of judgment. Here, this absence of judgement not only refers to the ~judgement of individuals, but the ~judgement of your surroundings in the present or future. When we judge our surroundings we formulate perception, and possibly expectations. Perception is a tricky (Biblically intrinsically sinful) thing. Imagine we have lenses over our eyes and essentially over our ears and senses, which, due to our fears, ego, experiences, past, beliefs and expectations, we judge everything as we must, in order for our reality to make *sense*.

To master the unknown, or the chaotic, one must decrease one's potential, or derivable amount of actions, as a result of chaos or the unknown occurring, down to zero, or as close to zero as possible, while still representing who you are, while keeping aware of the things you (truly) want. If we are going to talk about

Christianity, then one doesn't want anything, except to be what God wants them to be. Submission here is important, for if one admits their general inability, without God, in the past, naturally one would not be interested in their old facts and perceptions and fear: flesh. To give up, and to seek what God wants one to do: to serve, can be stuff that destiny is made of. To be certain you are in the right place, at the right time, with the right people, doing the right things: being the arrow that springs from the bow. How does this relate to mastering chaos? Well, if you're viewing surprises or chaos, through a Godly lens, which is to say, viewing the world , say, with the question what would Jesus do?, on your mind, the amount of reactions, you could say that one is allowed to have at this point, by virtue of only doing what Jesus would do, are dramatically reduced from what their quantity could be. This is convenient. For an identical Reader, who was not concerned with what God would want, or what Jesus would do, a reduction of possible reactions to chaos can be instead or also derived from *certainty*. Certainty about who one is, and what one wants.

If one can feel as if an arrow, already fired from a bow, one will meet chaos with a relatively small number of possible actions, based on your awareness of aspects of yourself, Reader: awareness of who you are and what you actually want. Such a person meets new situations and individuals with a sense that they were meant to speak with that person, or destined to do that thing. It is theoretically possible to Truly understand why a thing happens, however, one's understanding does not necessarily have to do with why a thing happens or does not.

While being who you are, by virtue of your actions, which cannot be contradictory with your "wants," (conceptualized as conditions for fulfillment), you must remember not to judge yourself, as well as everything else. For this to be achieved, once again, one must realize that it is not about conceptualizing or figuring out how to not judge (yourself), but simply the lack of judgement where aspects of yourself (and everything else), are concerned. This is done by living one's destiny: being the arrow, flying between the bow and the inevitable target or end. It is inevitable, or at least out of your control what happens, the only certainty we can have is that we are who we are (based on what we want), and that by virtue, essentially of doing our best to do that which our "gutt" tells us, which we stand to hear more often, and benefit from, more completely, the less superfluous brain functions are running simultaneously.

Conditions & Roses

With zero judgement, coupled with zero illusion of control over one's world, or future outcomes therein, one may be themselves, not simply ceasing to be themselves when things don't go their way, due to lack of expectations, and therefore failure, where no conditions for failure have been set. Mastering this gives one the ability to "stop and smell the roses." What this has always meant it seems, is the ability of a person to notice all the little (good) things. One will start noticing more and thinking more, and perhaps better, the less superfluous brain functions are running, like stress, doubt and worry.

Fulfillment is derived from actions, or fruits of one's labor, which grew from being one's self, at the right place, at the right time. If you can feel as the arrow, headed to it's target, having been projected this way in one's past, flying clearly, and certainly in one way, one can feel fulfillment, as a result of destiny.

Conditions which your actions must meet, in order to produce the unique, individual self fruit, are as follows. First, Your cumulative actions, which is to say, the total sum of your actions: who you are, must benefit others. Your actions must produce enough wealth to cover your basic human living needs. Next, the actions must have been fascinating: you were inclined to act, due to a personal interest in, or with the subject(s) involved in the actions. Also that you are inclined to find out more on said subjects, or on involved, or adjacent concepts and subjects and virtues etc... Finally, on the subject of fulfillment, ones actions must benefit from past, present, and future dots, found on the timeline of one's life. It is the case that no one individual has lived exactly the same life as another, but it is the idea here, for the sake of developing peace, that You are your actions, and that someone else could be you, if they had the same set of past actions. What would Jesus do? God is said to have set out a destiny for all. These destinies would be realized, and made unique by each individual, and their actions, if each individual simply allowed them to. Fear of death melts away, and is (hopefully not) replaced simply by fear of failure to continue Living properly. Death is the end to a finite story. Don't miss yours. Failure to live one's destiny, is an illusion, to someone traveling down their road, or down their path, as the arrow which has sprung from the bow.

In order to find which things we are uniquely suited for, we must consider the things we are best at, unfortunately possibly, due to virtue of repetition. Consider worrying. It is difficult to think of how one could incorporate worrying into their day to generate fulfillment. Therefore, worrying is dust. Personally, I realized that I had, and wanted to have teacher on my list. Eventually, through humility, I discovered who I was uniquely talented at teaching, and why. Things are not always as they seem. You can be.

Processing Power

You, Reader, need to realize yourself more and more, largely by omitting all the things that you now do, from your *List*, that do not represent you. Imagine waking up tomorrow Reader. Imagine that the last thing you did before falling asleep was make a new copy of your *List*. This new *List*, naturally, is composed of all the things which now represent you, based on your actions yesterday, and every other day. It is, a magic *List*... Yesterday, you, worried for a total of one hour about things which you have no control over. Say, that this was farely in line with the average amount you worried every day. IS A WORRIER appears on your *List*. In order to no longer do something, which you now are such an expert at, that you do it by reflex, you will require training. As it requires training to be strong, if you are weak.

Consider a saying in martial arts that if one does a thing 10 thousand times, then they will have mastered it: they will do that thing without thought. If you are 40 years old, you never worried one single time until you turned 10, at which point you worried for an hour a day, you will have mastered worrying at 37, if one hour of worry was comparable to throwing one punch, where doing a thing without thinking is concerned. This would mean that you would have started worrying about things involuntarily & masterfully, 3 years ago. If, Reader, you hypothesis that you sleep seven hours a day, and worry for 1, that is one third of your day that you cannot be consciously realizing your destiny. If one were to worry 1/24 of the time, it would be logical to submit that one were able similarly only living a maximum of 23/24 their potential, if ~worrier represents who you are, truly.

Do you feel butterflies in your stomach? Kill them by waiting.

Re ~Cap

As time goes on, and you venture to maintain your road, keep to the path and venture closer and closer to what you consider to be God's road. You will need to remember many things, and you will encounter many trials. Yet, it will in fact be these trials as a result of your new self, that shapes you into a better version of the person you want to be, instead of a child of chaos. As time goes on, and these trials start adding up, it is perhaps wise to envision yourself climbing up a stairway. This stairway takes effort to get up. It's tiring. And the steps are essentially made up of you. Realize that you are your own, perhaps only enemy. Step onward, and upward. Continuously overcome yourself. Getting up to the next step, will doubtlessly take effort: perseverance. To overcome yourself, is to generate experience. Keep proceeding in the right direction: in Your direction. With each step. The rewards of fulfillment evolve, while fulfillment becomes routine.

Part of what it is to have fulfillment, is to overcome obstacles in your way, to your destiny.

To re cap, never forget that you are never perfect. And that every day is a new challenging set of challenges. Perseverance will only make you stronger and more like yourself, through generating experience, so that you'll be able to better relate to yourself, and the public that you can, in fact, relate to. These folks will become identifiable, once you have identified yourself. Imagine you were to meet someone, and both of you could identify each other as someone they could relate to.

   Keep in mind, especially when it's late during the day, that a secret weapon of ours, Reader, is the *restart* a decent sleep provides. We should not necessarily go to sleep, then, if we are feeling as the arrow, for when we worry, say, about our actions later on, then, we can use our human-born ability to sleep.

'Till Next Time,

Reader